A

gift

honoring

Griffin

and

Carson

Gilchrist

Easy Crafts in **5** Steps

Easy Cloth Crafts in 5 Steps

Enslow Elementary
an imprint of

Enslow Publishers, Inc.
40 Industrial Road
Box 398
Berkeley Heights, NJ 07922
USA
http://www.enslow.com

Note to Teachers and Parents: Crafts are prepared using air-drying clay. Please follow package directions. Children may use color clay or they may paint using poster paint once clay is completely dry. The colors used in this book are suggestions. Children may use any color cloth, clay, cardboard, pencils, or paint they wish. Let them use their imaginations!

Enslow Elementary, an imprint of Enslow Publishers, Inc.
Enslow Elementary® is a registered trademark of Enslow Publishers, Inc.

Translated from the Spanish edition by Ian Grenzeback, edited by Susana C. Schultz, of Strictly Spanish, LLC.
Edited and produced by Enslow Publishers, Inc.

Library of Congress Cataloging-in-Publication Data

Llimós Plomer, Anna.
  [Tejidos. English]
  Easy cloth crafts in 5 steps / Anna Llimós.
    p. cm. — (Easy crafts in 5 steps)
  Summary: "Presents craft projects that are made with fabric that can be made in 5 steps"—Provided by publisher.
  Includes bibliographical references and index.
  ISBN-13: 978-0-7660-3084-8
  ISBN-10: 0-7660-3084-9
  1. Textile crafts—Juvenile literature. I. Title.
  TT699.L5813 2007
  746—dc22
                          2007004221

Originally published in Spanish under the title *Tejidos.*
Copyright © 2005 PARRAMÓN EDICIONES, S.A., - World Rights.
Published by Parramón Ediciones, S.A., Barcelona, Spain.
Text and development of the exercises: Anna Llimós
Photographs: Nos & Soto

Printed in Spain

10 9 8 7 6 5 4 3 2 1

To Our Readers: We have done our best to make sure all Internet Addresses in this book were active and appropriate when we went to press. However, the author and the publishers have no control over and assume no liability for the material available on those Internet sites or on other Web sites they may link to. Any comments or suggestions can be sent by e-mail to comments@enslow.com or to the address on the back cover.

Every effort has been made to locate all copyright holders of material used in this book. If any errors or omissions have occurred, corrections will be made in future editions of this book.

Contents

Little Fish

MATERIALS

Cloth scrap
Different colors of thin felt
Cotton balls
Black marker
White glue
Scissors

1 Draw two identical fish outlines on felt. Cut them out.

2 Cut out two pieces of cloth scrap. Glue them to half of each fish shape.

3 Glue the two fish shapes together along the edge. Leave the tail unglued. Stuff the fish with cotton balls. Glue the tail shut.

4

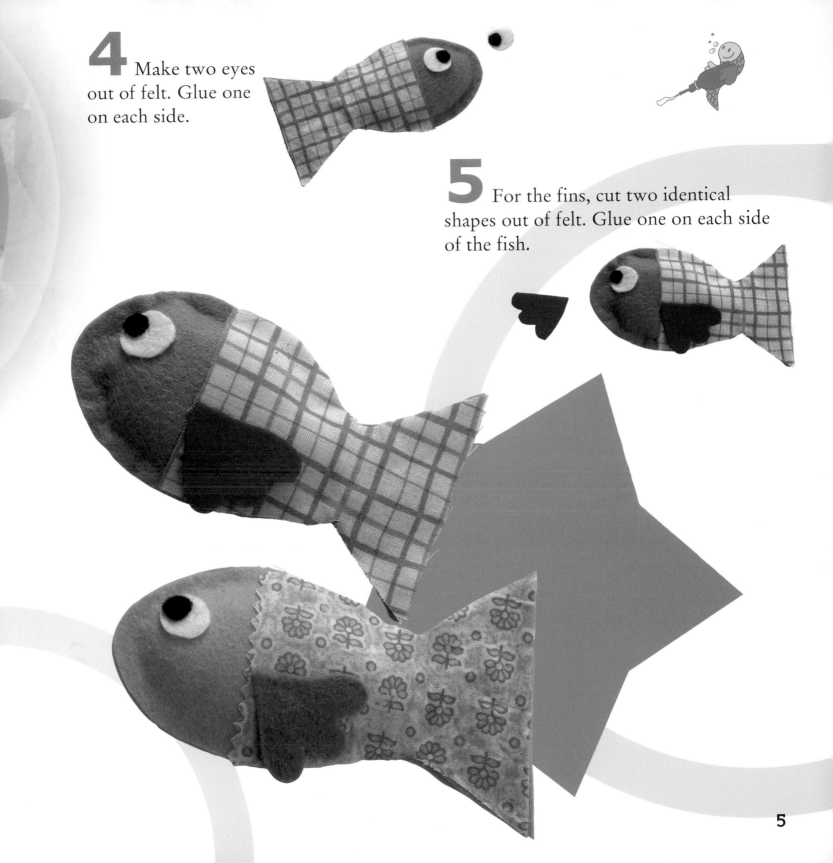

4 Make two eyes out of felt. Glue one on each side.

5 For the fins, cut two identical shapes out of felt. Glue one on each side of the fish.

Tray

MATERIALS

Stiff felt
Yarn
Stapler
White glue
Toothpick
Scissors
Marker
Ruler

1 Cut a square out of stiff felt. Draw a square inside it with the marker.

2 Glue some yarn on the line. If you use a toothpick to spread the glue, the yarn will not stick to your fingers.

3 Repeat the previous step with another color yarn. Cut off the excess yarn.

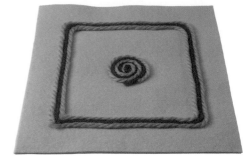

4 Finish decorating the felt square by gluing a spiral of both colors of yarn in the middle.

5 Staple the four corners of the square to make the sides of the tray.

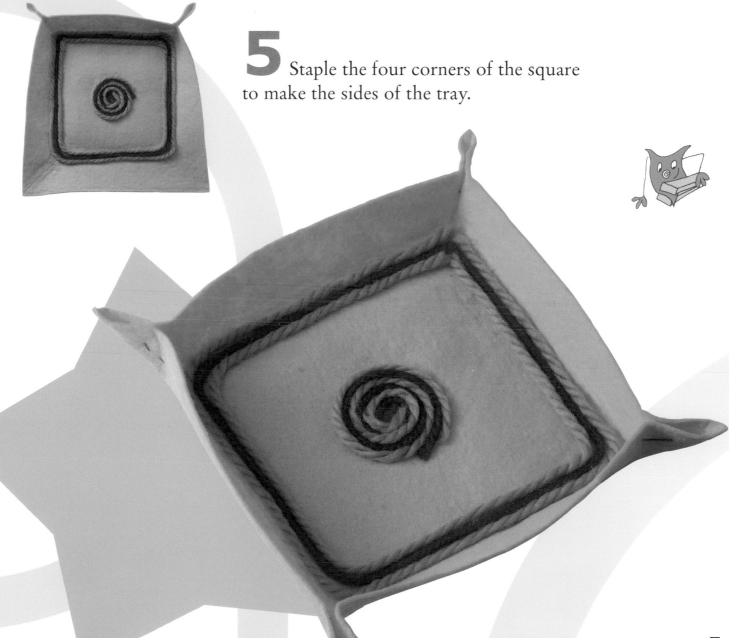

Turtle

MATERIALS

Kitchen sponge cloth
Thin felt
Marker
Stapler
Scissors

1 Draw the turtle's head, feet, and tail on sponge cloth. Cut them out.

2 Cut out a rectangle of sponge cloth. Staple it in the shape of a cylinder to the feet and tail. Now you have the shell!

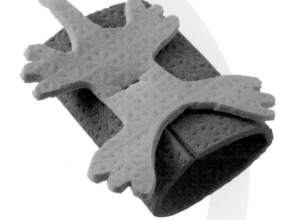

3 Turn it over and staple the shell at the tail end.

4 Staple the head to the front of the shell.

5 Finish shaping the front of the shell with two staples. Glue eyes made of felt to the turtle's head.

Clown

Thin felt
Stiff felt
Yarn
Thin wire
White glue
Scissors

1 For the body, cut out two strips of felt. Put a length of wire between them and glue the felt together.

2 Cut some shoes out of felt. Glue them to the bottom end. Decorate the part that will be the shirt with some strips of felt. For the head, cut two circles of the same size out of stiff felt.

3 Glue a felt nose and eyes and a yarn mouth on one felt circle. Glue the other circle to the back of the top of the body. Then glue the decorated circle on top.

10

4 For the arms, cut two thin strips of felt. Glue them together with a piece of wire in between. Glue felt hands at both ends.

5 Glue the arms behind the body. Make a cap out of felt and glue it on the head.

Flower

1 Cut out two rectangles of cloth.

2 Use packing tape to attach the two pieces of cloth to the dowel with one outside the other.

3 Cut a strip of felt as long as the dowel and a little wider at one end.

12

4 Wrap the dowel with the strip of felt, so that the wide part covers the packing tape. Glue the felt together.

5 Draw and cut two leaves out of felt. Glue them to the flower stem.

13

Purse

1 Cut a long rectangle out of burlap. With different colors of yarn, sew a burlap pocket onto one of the ends.

2 Fold over the rectangle, leaving one side longer for the flap. Sew the sides of the purse. Make some stitches around the flap to decorate it.

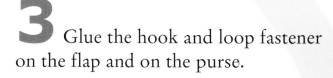

3 Glue the hook and loop fastener on the flap and on the purse.

4 For the strap, cut three pieces of yarn of different colors. Attach them to the purse with a knot at each end.

5 Finally, draw and cut a flower out of felt. Glue it on the pocket.

Necklace and Bracelet

MATERIALS

Yarn
Thin felt
Wood bead
Hook and loop fastener
White glue
Scissors

1 Cut three pieces of yarn. Fold a felt rectangle over the yarn and glue the edges.

2 Cut out another felt rectangle and another smaller one. Glue them on top in the center of the necklace.

3 For the clasp, tie the wood bead to one end of the yarn. Tie a loop at the other end.

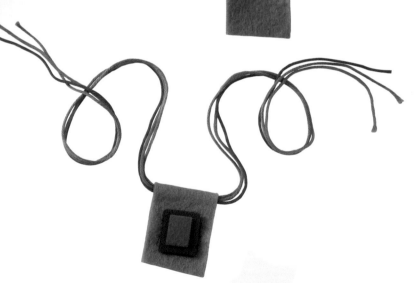

4 For the bracelet, cut a strip of felt the size of your wrist. Glue a piece of hook and loop fastener to each end.

5 Decorate the bracelet with little squares of felt.

Dog

MATERIALS

Thin felt
White glue
Scissors

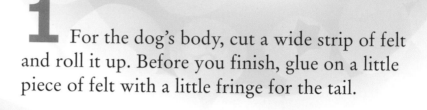

1 For the dog's body, cut a wide strip of felt and roll it up. Before you finish, glue on a little piece of felt with a little fringe for the tail.

2 For the legs, roll up four shorter and narrower strips of the same felt.

3 Make the head the same way you made the body. For the ears, glue a strip with rounded ends on top of it.

18

4 Make the dog's eyes, nose, and tongue out of felt. Glue everything onto the head.

5 To finish, glue the head and feet to the body.

19

Puppet

MATERIALS

Cloth scraps
Thin felt
Yarn
Toilet paper tube
Markers
White glue
Scissors

1 Cut a cloth scrap to cover the cardboard tube. Draw a face in the top middle part of the cloth scrap.

2 Cover the tube with the cloth with the face drawn on it.

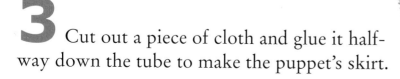

3 Cut out a piece of cloth and glue it halfway down the tube to make the puppet's skirt.

4 Cut out two strips of felt for the arms. Glue felt hands on the ends. Glue the arms to the puppet.

5 For the hair, cut several pieces of yarn. Tie them together in the middle and glue them onto the puppet's head.

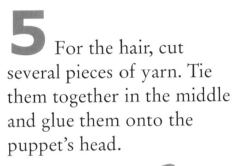

21

Owl

MATERIALS

Old pants pocket
(Ask permission first!)
Thin felt
Stapler
White glue
Scissors

1 For the beak, cut out a felt triangle and glue it to the pocket.

2 Use felt to make some big eyes. Glue them onto the pocket, above the beak.

3 Draw and cut two triangular ears out of felt. Staple them to the pocket.

22

4 For the wings, cut out two pieces of felt. Cut out two smaller pieces of felt. Give all the pieces some fringe.

5 Staple the two wings to the back of the pocket.

23

Felt Doll

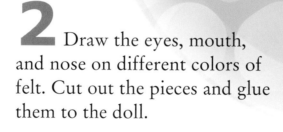

1 Draw the outline of a doll on the stiff felt and cut it out.

MATERIALS

Stiff felt
Thin felt
Yarn
Cloth scraps
Hook and loop fastener
Black marker
White glue
Scissors

2 Draw the eyes, mouth, and nose on different colors of felt. Cut out the pieces and glue them to the doll.

3 For the hair, cut different colors of yarn and tie them in the middle. Glue them to the doll's head.

4 Draw the shape of a shirt and pants on the cloth scrap. Cut them out. Put the hook and loop fastener on the back of each piece of clothing.

5 Dress the doll with the shirt and pants.

25

Pompom Key Ring

MATERIALS

Cardboard
Different colors of yarn
Scissors
Compass (to draw a circle)
Metal ring (for key ring)

1 Draw two identical rings on cardboard with a compass and cut them out. Make a cut in both of them.

2 Put the two rings together and wrap different colors of yarns around them. The cut you made will make it easier to pass the yarn through.

3 Stick the tip of the scissors between the two rings of cardboard and cut the yarn.

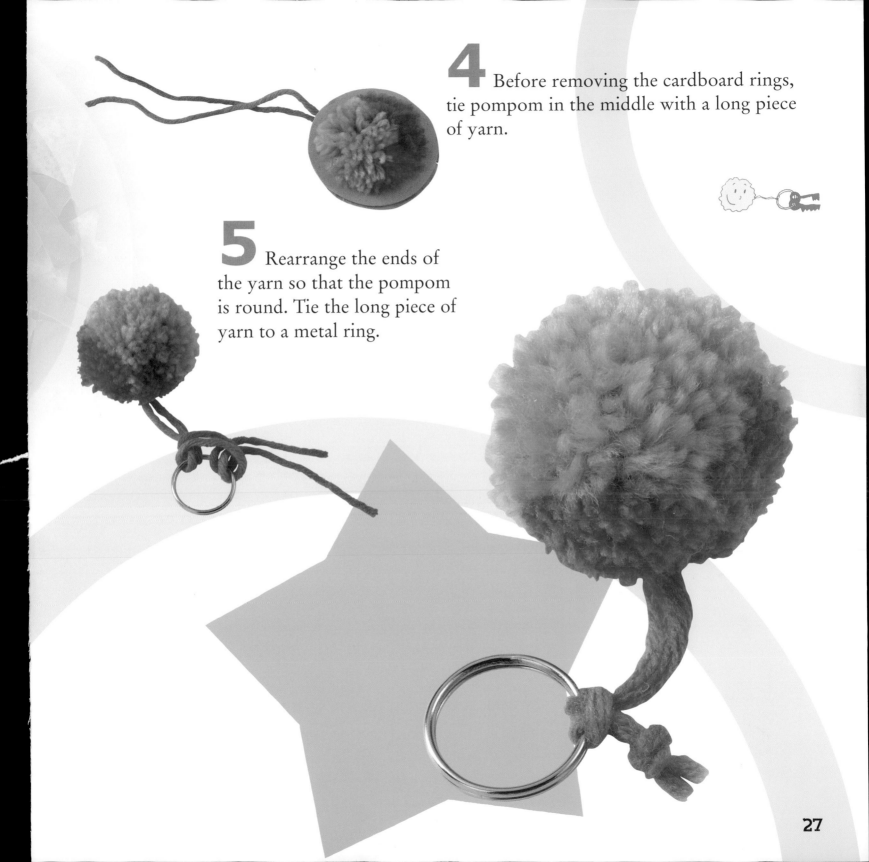

4 Before removing the cardboard rings, tie pompom in the middle with a long piece of yarn.

5 Rearrange the ends of the yarn so that the pompom is round. Tie the long piece of yarn to a metal ring.

Seagull

MATERIALS

Thin felt
Cloth scrap
Yarn
Stapler
White glue
Pencil
Scissors

1 For the seagull's body and head, draw and cut a shape like the one shown out of felt.

2 Roll the body up to the head. Staple it together along with yarn.

3 For the beak, cut a triangle out of felt and glue it on. Make the bird's eyes out of felt.

4 Glue two small triangles of cloth scrap to the wing tips.

5 Cut four clouds out of felt. Glue them to the yarn that supports the seagull.

Fabric Collage

1 For the sky, cover half of the poster board with cloth scrap.

MATERIALS

Poster board
Different colors of cloth scrap
Thin felt
Black marker
White glue
Scissors

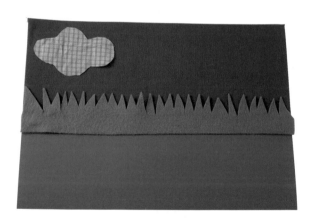

2 Draw and cut a patch of grass out of felt. Cut a cloud out of cloth scrap. Glue them to the poster board.

3 Draw the outline of a car on a piece of cloth scrap and cut it out. Glue it in the middle of the poster board.

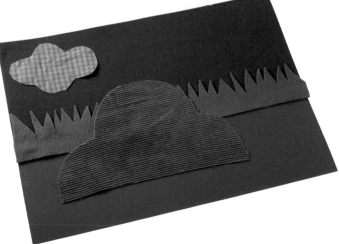

30

4 For the windows, cut out two pieces of cloth scrap. Cut wheels out of felt. Glue everything onto the car.

5 Make a stop light with felt and glue it next to the car.

Read About

Books

Blanchette, Peg, and Terri Thibault. *Really Cool Felt Crafts*. Charlotte, Ver.: Williamson Pub., 2002.

McAllister, Buff. *Sewing with Felt: Learn Basic Stitches to Create More Than 60 Colorful Projects*. Honesdale, Penn.: Boyds Mills Press, 2003.

Wallace, Mary. *I Can Make That! Fantastic Crafts for Kids*. Toronto, Canada: Maple Tree Press, 2005.

Internet Addresses

Crafts for Kids at Enchanted Learning
<http://www.enchantedlearning.com/crafts/>

Kids Craft Weekly
<http://www.kidscraftweekly.com/>

Index

Easy to Hard